Cursive handwriting for kids

This book belongs to

Bruce Gibson

Indroduction & Tips

Learning cursive writing is a key milestone in a child's academic journey. This is an exciting time, but can also be a little daunting for the child. To make learning as smooth and effective as possible, here are ten top tips:

1. Body basics

Good posture is important for cursive writing. Encourage children to sit with their feet flat on the floor, their back straight (no heads on the table) and relaxed shoulders.

2. Think Ink

Although children usually write in pencil at school, it can be useful for them to start cursive handwriting with felt tips and gel pens, which have a nice, fluid delivery of ink.

3. B prepared

If your child is using a pencil, the softer B pencils are generally easier to write with as they move more fluently across the page.

4. Let loose

Don't stick to practising on paper. Get children to practise their letters in other mediums, such as tracing them in the air, in sand with a stick or on another person's back with their finger. Make learning fun and creative.

5. Get a grip

Keep an eye on the child's pencil grip. It's important that the pad of the thumb connects with the pencil. If the side or tip of the thumb touches, it closes up the hand and restricts the flow of movement.

6. Let's twist

The child may find cursive writing easier if their paper is at an angle. You can turn the page up to 45 degrees in either direction.

7. Left learning

Left-handed children may have more trouble as they push the pencil across the paper, rather than pulling it. A writing slope can be beneficial for left-handed children as it helps them to see their writing.

8. Teaching terms

To help your child at home, ask how handwriting is being taught at school: for example, do they refer to entry and exit strokes, flicks or tails? It's important to use consistent language so you can give your child effective instructions.

9. Method matching

Handwriting styles vary from school to school, so it's important to be consistent and ask children to write 'f's, 'r's, 'k's and other letters that tend to vary in style the same way at home and in the classroom.

10. Easy does it

Finally, keep handwriting practice light and fun. Nagging your child about their writing will only reduce their enthusiasm. Always give praise where it's due and try not to hover over them – they need time to fully experience each task.

Part 1: Learning letters

Trace the dotted letters on the top line, then write the letters in the remaining space

because

Bruce

Redeem you

m m m m m

m

m m m m

m

n n n n n n

n

n n n n n

n

p p p p p p p

P P P P P P

u *u* *u* *u* *u* *u*

U *U* *U* *U* *U*

uu uu uu uu uu

u

w w w w

w

Part 2:
Simple Words

Trace the dotted words on the
top line, then write them
in the remaining space

(By the way, you're doing brilliantly!)

boy boy boy boy boy

What do you call a dinosaur that is sleeping?

girl girl girl girl girl

A dino-snore

baby baby baby baby

Why did the teddy bear say no to dessert?

food food food food

Because she was stuffed

moon moon moon

What did one plate say to the other plate?

hand hand hand

Dinner is on me

glad glad glad glad

Why did the student eat his homework?

name name name

Because the teacher said it was a piece of cake

pony pony pony

Why did the kid cross the playground?

truck truck truck

To get to the other slide

late late late late late

Why was 6 afraid of 7?

wind wind wind

Because 7, 8, 9

nice nice nice nice

What kind of tree fits in your hand?

doll doll doll doll

A palm tree

candy *candy* *candy*

Why did the cookie go to the hospital?

use *use* *use* *use* *use*

Because he felt crummy

your your your your

Why was the baby strawberry crying?

away away away

Because her mom and dad were in a jam

best best best best best

What did the little corn say to the mama corn?

lunch lunch lunch

Where is pop corn?

club club club club

What falls in winter but never gets hurt?

what what what

Snow

drive *drive* *drive*

How do we know that the ocean is friendly?

very *very* *very* *very*

It waves

each each each each

How does a scientist freshen her breath?

tree tree tree tree tree

farm   *farm*   *farm*

How can you tell a vampire has a cold?

soon soon soon soon

He starts coffin

goat goat goat goat

How do you make an octopus laugh?

riding riding riding

With ten-tickles

above *above* *above*

What did the nose say to the finger?

become *become* *become*

Quit picking on me

cattle cattle cattle

Why couldn't the pony sing a lullaby?

dinner dinner dinner

She was a little hoarse

everyone everyone

Why didn't the skeleton go to the dance?

family family family

He had no body to dance with

ground ground ground

Why did the banana go to the doctor?

heard heard heard

Because it wasn't peeling well

inches   inches   inches

What do you call a funny mountain?

Juice   Juice   Juice

Hill-arious

Kitten Kitten Kitten

Why do bees have sticky hair?

Large Large Large

Because they use a honeycomb

Merry Merry Merry

Why did Johnny throw the clock out of the window?

noise   noise   noise

Because he wanted to see time fly

Orange Orange Orange

What do you call an old snowman?

Picture Picture Picture

Water

Queen Queen Queen

What time should you go to the dentist?

Running Running

Tooth hurty

Shield Shield Shield

Why did they quit giving tests at the zoo?

Teacher Teacher Teacher

Because it was full of cheetahs

Under Under Under

What room can no one enter?

Value Value Value

A mushroom

Winter Winter Winter

Why couldn't the pirate learn the alphabet?

Xray Xray Xray

Because he was always lost at C

Zapping   *Zapping*

What are the strongest days of the week?

yesterday   *yesterday*

Saturday and Sunday. Every other day is a weekday

remember remember

What goes tick-tock and woof-woof?

everybody everybody

A watchdog

Literacy   Literacy

What do monsters turn on in the summer?

astronaut   astronaut

Their scare conditioner

Different   Different

Why do shoemakers go to heaven?

Suddenly Suddenly

Because the have good soles

President *President*

Want me to tell you a joke about pizza?

Sentence *Sentence*

Sorry, it is too cheesy

probably   probably

Why was the broom late?

important important

It overswept

happiness   happiness

Why did the golfer wear two pairs of pants?

favorite   favorite

In case he got a hole in one

Countries   Countries

What word starts with E and has only one letter in it?

Beautiful   Beautiful

Envelope

attention, attention

What do you give a sick lemon?

transform, transform

Lemon aid

ambition *ambition*

What animal is best at hitting a ball?

ingenious *ingenious*

A bat

medicine *medicine*

What did the blanket say to the bed?

maximum *maximum*

I've got you covered

Encounter Encounter

What kind of snack do you have during a scary movie?

Dominate Dominate

Ice cream

I am great at writing

Why do tigers have stripes?

Bring on part three!

So they don't get spotted

Part 3: Sentences

Carefully read the joke or riddle, then write it in the space below

(Has anyone told you you're amazing at handwriting? Well you are!)

What do you call it
when a dinosaur
crashes his car?

Tyrannosaurus Wrecks

What gets wetter and wetter the more they dry?

Towels

What is big, green and plays a lot of tricks?

Prank-enstein

What are full of
holes but still
hold water?

Sponges

Why does the
sun have to
go to school?

To get brighter

Where do cows go for some entertainment?

The mooooo-vies

Who is the person
that everyone has to
take his hat off too?

The barber

What creatures are smarter than talking parrots?

Spelling bees

What never asks questions but is often answered?

Doorbells

What's the worst thing about throwing a party in space?

You have to planet

What belongs to you but other people use it more than you?

Your name

What was the snake's favorite subject at school?

Hissstory

What word becomes shorter when you add two letters to it?

Short

What did the
pencil say to the
other pencil?

You're looking sharp

What has to be broken before you can use them?

Eggs

What is the best day of the week to go to the beach?

Sunday

Where does Friday
come before
Thursday?

In the dictionary

Why should you always take a pencil to bed?

To draw the curtains

What is so delicate that saying its name breaks it?

Silence

What did the triangle say to the circle?

- - - - - - - - -

- - - - - - - - -

- - - - - - - - -

- - - - - - - - -

You're pointless

- - - - - - - - -

Which word in the
dictionary is spelled
incorrectly?

Incorrectly

What do you call
a bear with no
socks on?

Bare-foot

What did the beach say when the tide came in?

Long time, no sea

What is the best
thing to do if a
bull charges you?

Pay the bull

What is an astronaut's favorite place on a computer?

The space bar

Why did the bumble
bee put honey under
his pillow?

To have sweet dreams

What is something you will never see again?

Yesterday

What did the outlaw get when he stole a calendar?

Twelve months

What are two things you cannot have for breakfast?

Lunch and dinner

What did one
potato chip say
to the other?

Shall we go for a dip?

Can you guess
what is at the
end of a rainbow?

The letter W

Why did the boy bury his flashlight?

_____

- -

_____

- -

_____

- -

_____

- -

_____

The batteries died

_____

- -

_____

What type of cheese is made backwards?

Edam

Why do birds
fly south in
the winter?

It's too far to walk

If two's company and three's a crowd, what are four and five?

Nine

What did the little tree say to the big tree?

Leaf me alone

What did the tree wear to the pool party?

Swimming trunks

Who deserves a huge treat for mastering handwriting?

You do!

Made in the USA
Columbia, SC
13 January 2019